P9-BZB-525

Praise for *Homer's Odyssey*

"A must-read for anyone who has ever loved an animal."
—Fredericksburg *Free Lance-Star*

"Heartwarming and entertaining."

—PEOPLE Pets

"Delightful . . . This lovely human-feline memoir . . . is sure to warm the hearts of all pet lovers."

—Library Journal

"A wonderful story celebrating the profound bond that can form between feline and human. *Homer's Odyssey* is an inspiring read, and a perfect holiday gift for any cat lovers on your list."

—Feline Wellness

"I am certain it would be impossible to meet Homer without falling in love with him and it is just as difficult to read this loving account without coming away with a renewed faith in the unique bond that can sometimes arise between two alien species. Gwen Cooper writes with humor, with wit, with candor, and most of all with irresistible warmth for this astonishing little feline who will steal your heart."

—Jeffrey Moussaieff Masson,
***New York Times* bestselling author of**
***The Nine Emotional Lives of Cats* and**
When Elephants Weep

Praise for *Love Saves the Day*

"Once again Gwen Cooper shines her light on the territory that defines the human/animal bond. In *Love Saves the Day*, she creates an emotional landscape so beautifully complete that we can't help but share in the heartbreaks and triumphs of her characters, regardless of their species. That, in itself, is a reason to stand up and cheer."

—JACKSON GALAXY, star of *My Cat From Hell* and author of *Cat Daddy*

"[A] poignant tale . . . [Gwen Cooper] once again demonstrates her compassionate fluency in felinespeak and proves equally adept at conveying compels human emotions with flair and sensitivity."

—*Booklist*

"Unforgettably moving . . . a hard one to put down."

—*Modern Cat*

"If you are the Most Important Person to a cat, you will hold them much tighter by the book's end. If you don't have a cat, Prudence will have surreptitiously lured you into the danger zone: Falling in love with a cat because they need family too."

—*The Vancouver Sun*

HOMER AND THE HOLIDAY MIRACLE

OTHER CAT STORIES BY GWEN COOPER

Homer's Odyssey:
A Fearless Feline Tale, or How I Learned About
Love and Life with a Blind Wonder Cat

Homer:
The Ninth Life of a Blind Wonder Cat

Love Saves the Day

My Life in a Cat House:
True Tales of Love, Laughter, and Living with Five Felines

The Curl Up with a Cat Tale series

"I Choo-Choo-Choose You!"

"Stop Trying to Make Fetch Happen"

"The Picasso of Pee"

"Cat Carrier Tango"

"THEM! *A Story in Five Parts*"

"Fanny Trouble"

HOMER AND THE HOLIDAY MIRACLE

A TRUE STORY

GWEN COOPER

BenBella Books, Inc.
Dallas, TX

Copyright ©2018 by Gwen Cooper

BenBella Books, Inc.
10440 N. Central Expressway, Suite 800 | Dallas, TX 75231
www.benbellabooks.com
Send feedback to feedback@benbellabooks.com

Printed in the United States of America
10 9 8 7 6 5 4 3 2 1

Library of Congress Cataloging-in-Publication Data is available upon request.
978-1-946885-7-84 (print)
978-1-946885-8-21 (e-book)

Editing by Leah Wilson
Copyediting by Karen Wise
Proofreading by Cape Cod Compositors, Inc.
Text design and composition by Silver Feather Design
Cover design by Sarah Avinger
Printed by Lake Book Manufacturing

Distributed to the trade by Two Rivers Distribution,
an Ingram brand
www.tworiversdistribution.com

Special discounts for bulk sales (minimum of 25 copies) are available. Please contact Aida Herrera at aida@benbellabooks.com.

*For the "Homer's Heroes" in animal rescue,
who work tirelessly to make sure every cat and dog
has the home they deserve—at the holidays,
and all year round*

A candle is a small thing. But one candle can light another. And see how its own light increases, as a candle gives its flame to the other.

—MOSHE DAVIS

AUTHOR'S NOTE

Maybe you've already heard about the little, five-pound black cat who was the star of the internationally bestselling memoir *Homer's Odyssey: A Fearless Feline Tale, or How I Learned About Love and Life with a Blind Wonder Cat*—the blind, heroic Daredevil who saved his human mom's life the night he chased off an intruder who'd broken into their home while they slept and made his way into their bedroom; the online phenom with more than a million followers on social media who's become the face of special-needs rescue animals the world over; the cat who lived a life of adventure and joy despite early predictions that he would always be "timid" and "dependent."

The cat who proved beyond any shadow of a doubt that love isn't something you see with your eyes.

Homer was, in many ways, a miraculous cat. But of all the miracles and wonders he performed over the years, perhaps the greatest was simply that he'd managed to survive at all. He'd very nearly been euthanized when he was only a few weeks old, simply because nobody wanted to take a chance on a kitten who was different. I'll admit that I also had my doubts at first. Homer came into my life at the worst possible moment—when I'd just lost my fiancé, my home, and my job, all within weeks of each other. How could I possibly take care of a blind kitten when I could barely take care of myself?

AUTHOR'S NOTE

I realize now that it's precisely during those times in our lives—the ones we describe as being the "worst possible"—when miracles are likeliest to occur. After all, if they didn't happen when we needed them most, they wouldn't be miracles in the first place.

Homer taught me that. And he taught me many other true and good things, without which my life would have been infinitely poorer.

I've been lucky enough to love and live with many wonderful cats and dogs over the years, and I can't imagine what my life would have been like if I hadn't known any one of them. Still, my relationship with Homer was unique. Perhaps it was inevitable that he and I became almost preternaturally close. He was only three or four weeks old when I adopted him—little more than a wee ball of black kitten fuzz who followed my footsteps so closely, as he learned to navigate his new home without the benefit of sight, that if I happened to stop short, his tiny nose ran right into my ankle. Homer listened closely to the varying tones and inflections of my voice for any clue I could give him about his surroundings—and, of course, I paid very close attention to him and his needs, especially at first. It got to the point where our hyper-awareness of each other was constant and unconscious—where *not* knowing what the other was doing or feeling at any given moment was the thing that would have required effort. Our closeness was a permanent and defining feature of our relationship, long after Homer had learned to get around even new and unfamiliar spaces all on his own and no longer needed me to be his see-ing-eye human.

My husband, Laurence (a longtime comic-book fan), who came into our lives seven years later, used to say that Homer was my "sym-biote." When I was happy, Homer rejoiced. If I was in a bad mood, Homer also took to moping around the house.

It was hard to stay in a bad mood for very long, though, with Homer around. He loved getting into the kind of trouble that could always coax a laugh out of me—scaling a pair of jeans hanging in the closet to reach some forbidden top shelf where I'd stashed a trove of cat toys, or "hiding" in plain sight in the middle of the floor (being blind, Homer thought *quiet* and *invisible* were the same thing) as he prepared to spring out at me in a "surprise" attack. Despite those early predictions that he might never be more than a "scaredy-cat," Homer lived a life of courage and joy—and became proof positive, to all who knew him, that nobody can ever tell you what your potential is.

If you already know Homer, you'll get to catch up with some old acquaintances through the pages of this tale. You'll also meet a couple of furry new additions to our household, which has continued to grow and flourish since Homer's story was published and he was first introduced to the world.

If you're a newcomer, we're delighted that you've chosen to spend some of your holiday season with our family. More than just about anything else he loved—and he fiercely loved many, many things—Homer's greatest joy was making new friends.

HOMER AND THE HOLIDAY MIRACLE

When most people think about cats at the holidays, their thoughts are more apt to turn to mischief than miracles. If you're a cat person yourself (and I'm guessing you are), then you don't need to see any one of dozens of viral videos to know what cats will do to a Christmas tree—the gleeful way they smash ornaments, tangle up lights, shred carefully handcrafted paper trimmings, or simply knock the whole tree down altogether. And heaven help your poor angelic tree topper—perhaps handed down in your family for generations—if it falls into the pitiless clutches of your feline friend.

Homer—the blind, black cat I adopted as a very young kitten in 1997—destroyed exactly one Christmas tree in just such a fashion. It was the first I had allowed myself to indulge in after moving out of my parents' house. After its destruction, with many a regretful sigh, I gave up on the idea of having a holiday tree of my very own. I learned to make do with a single strand of multihued lights festooned around the living room ceiling—although achieving even that much holiday cheer was something of a chore with Homer around. He'd follow behind me, yanking the string of lights down as fast as I could fasten it up, twining the lights (and his body along with them) into increasingly complex knots until finally, my patience exhausted, I'd yell, "Homer! *Enough* already!"

Then there was the year when I made the fatal error of leaving unattended for one minute (*one* minute, I tell you!) the pile of holiday gifts I'd spent two hours painstakingly wrapping. I returned to find what looked like a crime scene, or the wreckage left behind by a school of paper-loving piranhas that had somehow made it from water to land. Every year after that—in a gesture I made with profound love, but also with the certain knowledge that I was allowing Homer to shake me down in what was basically an old-school protection racket—I'd bury a catnip toy in some tissue paper, place it carefully in the kind of flip-top box Homer could easily open, and wrap the whole thing in colorful gift paper topped with ribbons.

I liked to joke about Homer's "superpowers"—the off-the-charts hearing that allowed him to catch buzzing flies (flies he couldn't even see!) in midair; the keen sense of smell capable of detecting his favorite deli turkey even through four or five layers of wax paper and plastic bags. So it was no surprise that Homer's sensitive nose could detect the scent of catnip lurking in the depths of his holiday gift box, and I think he enjoyed tearing the box, paper, and ribbon to pieces almost as much as he loved the catnip-laced prize itself. In any event, this seasonal bribe usually ensured the safety of all my other wrapped gifts—although I still had to guard my spool of ribbon, using my whole body to shield it, as carefully as the Secret Service guards the president.

There's plenty of feline mischief in the tale I'm about to tell, because Homer was, above all things, a mischievous, fun-loving cat. Ultimately, though, this is the story of a bona fide holiday miracle that happened in our own home, before our own eyes.

Before we go back, however, to five years ago when all this happened, I first have to take you back a bit farther—to just over two thousand years ago. Most people know the story of Christmas and the idea of Christmastime as a joyous season when miracles abound. But not as many know the story of Hanukkah, which typically falls near Christmas on the calendar. Both stories are important to this one.

Long ago, in the second century BCE, Greek forces occupied the land of Israel and persecuted the Jewish people cruelly for many, many years. Finally, a man named

Judah from a small village called Modi'in joined with his five brothers to lead a rebellion against the Greeks. His "army" was seven thousand untrained peasants pitted against a Greek contingent of fifty thousand professional soldiers. The Greeks came to call Judah the "Maccabee" (Greek for "hammer") for the fierce strength and courage he showed in the face of such overwhelming odds. Eventually, there was a decisive battle at the Great Temple in Jerusalem and the Jewish rebels won, driving the Greeks from Israel for good.

That victory came at a price, however, with the holy Temple sustaining heavy damage. Worst of all, there was only enough oil left to keep the Eternal Flame—sacred symbol of a living God that could never, ever be allowed to go out—burning for one more day. It would take at least eight days for new oil to be made and sanctified, and it was simply impossible for one day's worth of oil to last that long. Miraculously, though—without any additional oil or fuel to keep it going— the Eternal Flame burned for all eight of those days. This became known as the Miracle of the Lights, and it's commemorated every year as the holiday of Hanukkah.

It was a small miracle, perhaps, as such things go. Not quite as dramatic as a burning bush or the Red Sea parting. Still, it's a reminder that even a small flame can shed a great light.

This story—the one you're about to read—is the story of such a miracle. It's the story of a very small cat who had, we were told, only a little light left in him. Just enough to burn for another two weeks at most, if we were lucky.

And yet, that small light would grow into a great one. It was a light that—in defiance of all logic or medical science—continued to burn, bright and fierce.

And it didn't burn for only two weeks. It would burn for the better part of another year.

It was early December 2012 when Homer, who was then fifteen years old, fell over in a faint one afternoon while we were playing a round of that ever-popular game, Change The Bedsheets. In a panic, Laurence and I rushed him to the vet's office. Ultimately, Homer was diagnosed with acute liver failure, his liver values (the level of the toxins, typically filtered out by the liver, that were present in his blood) being *fifteen hundred* percent higher than what was normal for a cat. "Incompatible with life" was the phrase the doctor used the next day, when the blood work came back from the lab, in explaining Homer's numbers to me.

Treatment options, even the aggressive ones, were limited—and in any case had been emphatically ruled out by Homer himself, the absolute worst patient in our clinic's thirty-year history of dealing with hostile felines (or so the vet techs assured me as they tended to their wounds).

Brought in nearly unconscious, my four-pound blind cat had still managed to fend

9

off—with razor-sharp claws and roars of fury so loud they'd disrupted the entire hospital and every animal in it—one doctor and two experienced vet techs for the better part of forty minutes. They hadn't allowed me to accompany Homer into the emergency area but finally called me in to calm him down long enough to sedate him and draw blood for testing before sending us home.

Most cats, of course, don't have to be fully sedated merely to get a blood test. What can I say? Homer always *was* special.

He was also, usually, an exceptionally friendly cat. Homer's eagerness to engage new people and make new pals had become the stuff of legend. But the vet's office had always held a stark terror for Homer—and, despite everything I'd done to try to make things better for him (and for Homer's battle-weary doctors, who really were only trying to help), things had only grown worse as the years passed. So when the doctor, having called to discuss Homer's test results, suggested as tactfully as possible that Homer was "unlikely to benefit from a hospital environment," I was in no position to argue the point.

Instead of any intensive or invasive treatment, the vet prescribed a course of medication that could be mixed in with Homer's food—if Homer could even be coaxed into eating, which the doctor seemed to feel was unlikely under the circumstances. The medicine might buy Homer a few more days, perhaps another two weeks at the very most. Given the level of toxins in his blood, there was no plausible explanation for how he was still alive right *now*, and any long-term prospects seemed doubtful, if not downright impossible. That Homer could even pick up his head and walk around was an amazing accomplishment—and the vet warned that I should expect to see very minimal activity from Homer over the course of whatever few days he had left.

I had gone out to grab a quick sandwich with Laurence when I got the doctor's call on my cell, and I was in tears by the time we got home with what was left of our half-eaten lunch in carryout bags. Homer was dying—he was *dying*—and I'd left him to go get a sandwich. The twenty minutes I'd been gone suddenly seemed like an infinity of time—time during which anything, *anything* at all, might have happened.

I don't know what I expected to find upon our return, but the vivid images my imagination readily supplied did nothing to comfort me.

The first to greet us when we opened the front door were the two kittens, now ten months old, who we'd adopted back in April to keep Homer company after losing his two older sisters. Clayton was our "tripod" (so called because he had only one hind leg), a coal-black, roly-poly mush of a cat with a high squeaky voice, an endlessly fun-loving disposition, and a double dose of admiration for his big brother, Homer—tiny Homer who was, for all his small stature, still the biggest cat Clayton could remember ever having seen.

Fanny was his littermate, a sleek, sweet-natured beauty with Clayton's same ebony fur, although Fanny's was perhaps a touch glossier. Fanny didn't like to roughhouse as much as her brothers did, but she'd been nothing but gentle and respectful with Homer—and I knew that her affectionate patience had been good for his spirits.

Homer had been an unwilling big brother at first but, over the past few months, Clayton and Fanny's kittenish high spirits had coaxed him back to all his youthful playfulness. Lately, he'd developed an especial fondness for crouching down and "hiding," then leaping upon Clayton in sudden ambushes. And despite Homer never having grasped the concept of vision well enough to be much good at hiding, Clayton—who was the dearest little boy in the world—wasn't nearly as clever as Homer. It tended to make for a pretty even match.

When we entered the apartment now, the kittens were waiting for us at the door, but Homer was nowhere to be seen. My heart dropped into my stomach. "Homer?" I called anxiously. "Homer-Bear, where are you?"

With the feline equivalent of a victory whoop, Homer leapt from the kitchen into the entry hall of our apartment, landing directly atop an unsuspecting Clayton. *Gotcha!*

Clayton promptly pulled out from under Homer's weight and wiggled his one-legged backside, preparing to launch a counteroffensive. But Homer was already distracted by the aroma wafting temptingly from the take-out bags Laurence was carrying.

Hooray—you have food! He brought his rapidly twitching nose in for a closer inspection. *What are we having?*

15

The common thread uniting all the great Christmas stories is the telling of wondrous, miraculous events. Not one of them is a story about something that *could* have happened, but then didn't. *A Christmas Carol* isn't that much-beloved redemption tale about three ghosts who *don't* show up. *Rudolph the Red-Nosed Reindeer* isn't the parable of a uniquely gifted reindeer who opted *not* to guide Santa's sleigh one foggy Christmas Eve. Even the story of the first Hanukkah isn't that one about the seven thousand ragtag rebels who stared down the barrel of overwhelming odds and then said to themselves, *Meh . . . why bother?*

But, for us, the wondrous, miraculous thing that happened five years ago wasn't so much something that *did* happen, but rather something that was supposed to happen—that we were told, down to a medical certainty, was absolutely *going* to happen—but that ultimately never came to pass. At least, it didn't come to pass for so long that, by the time it did, even the most rational among our family and friends had come to laugh off "medical certainty" as primitive superstition, and to believe that the only true certainty in life is that there are no certainties.

What I'm trying to say is that, back in December 2012, the absence of news was the very best news we could have hoped for. And that was exactly what we got.

For the first time ever, I dreaded the unmistakable signs of the holidays' approach—the glitter of shimmering Christmas decorations overtaking Manhattan, the fairyland glow of cunningly decorated shop windows, the colorful pile of holiday cards and newsletters piling up on the kitchen counter. Wrapping Homer's customary catnip holiday gift in one of the flip-top boxes he so loved to pry open, I wondered if there was even a point to it. The first night of Hanukkah was four days away, and the last night was twelve. Would Homer still be here when we lit the last candle? Christmas was three weeks distant, and three weeks had suddenly become a lifetime—*more* than a lifetime, in fact. It seemed certain that Homer would be gone well before Christmas Eve.

At this thought, my eyes filled with tears and my hands grew so shaky that I couldn't get the wrapping paper onto the gift box. I told myself that I'd get to it later, but days went by and I never did.

Over the next few days, I kept waiting for Homer to slow down, for the high gloss of his black fur to dull, for him to stop cavorting with Clayton and Fanny, or trailing me from room to room while his little paws made a cheerful *clip-clop* on the tile floor. I waited for his favorite toys to begin gathering the dust of neglect, for the kittens to wonder anxiously why their beloved big brother—their tormentor and role model, whose every movement fascinated them to no end—refused to get up and play. I waited for the tinges of yellow in Homer's ears and gums—the easy-to-spot external sign of his jaundiced liver—to turn an angry, unmistakable egg-yolk gold.

And yet, none of the things I waited for took place. Not one—except, if I'm being strictly truthful, the yellow hue in Homer's ears did seem to deepen, just a little. Maybe. If you were looking closely.

If anything, Homer seemed positively rejuvenated in those first few days after his diagnosis. But that wasn't possible, I told myself sternly. The evidence of my own two eyes was the last thing I should be putting any trust in; I was only seeing what I wanted to see. The numbers were the numbers. They were facts—they were *certainties*. When the vet had said that Homer's numbers were "incompatible with life," I'd understood exactly what she'd meant: On paper, Homer was already gone. The most surprising thing about all the ruckus he'd caused at the hospital was that, with numbers like his, Homer should have been too weak even to twitch his ears—much less fend off three professional animal handlers who had at least a hundred and twenty pounds on him apiece.

Still, I couldn't help noticing what looked like an extra swagger in Homer's sleek panther prowl, one that hadn't been there before we'd gone to the vet's office. And the kittens, far from being unhappy, seemed even more besotted with Homer than usual, an extra gleam of adoration—not anxiety—shining in their wide eyes. Perhaps his victory over the hapless crew at the animal hospital (that day had felt far from "victorious" to me, but undoubtedly Homer saw things much differently) had roused Homer's fighting spirit, calling a retired, grizzled warrior back into the fray. I imagined him telling the story to Clayton and Fanny by the glow of a hallway nightlight, their eyes agog as Homer wove his yarn of fighting three giants into submission—all at the same time! *The thing is,* I pictured him saying with a cool, casual flick of a single gleaming claw, *you have to show these people who's boss.*

It was just before sundown on the first night of Hanukkah, four days after our emergency room visit, when the vet called to see how Homer was doing. I was in the kitchen, digging through our hopelessly cluttered "junk" drawer for menorah candles, while keeping my eyes peeled for any fuzzy interlopers who might make an attempt on the preparations for our holiday meal.

"You may have noticed a sharp decrease in Homer's appetite," the vet said, after we'd exchanged greetings. "The conundrum with cats who have liver problems is that it's super important for them to keep eating, but it's usually a struggle to get any food into them. I can prescribe an appetite stimulant, if you think that might help."

Just that afternoon, Homer had polished off an entire roasted chicken breast all by himself. Laurence had made it, intending it for his own lunch. But Homer pawed so pleadingly at Laurence's leg upon smelling the freshly cooked meat that Laurence wasn't able to resist giving him a few little bites. Neither of us was very good at saying no to anything Homer wanted at that point, and so the little bites turned into bigger chunks, and the number of bigger chunks kept growing, until Homer had wolfed the whole thing down to the bone.

Laurence was forced to content himself with the vegetables he'd prepared as a side, sighing a bit wistfully as he watched Homer daintily clean his face and whiskers once the chicken was gone.

That full chicken breast had been eaten just *after* Homer's usual lunchtime repast of canned cat food—his bowl was shining, he'd licked it so clean—along with an entire tin of sardines we'd gotten as a backup in case Homer's everyday food hadn't appealed to him. And then there was that bowlful of the Kitten Chow I'd bought as a tempting last resort (Kitten Chow being the only food that had reliably made Homer's older sisters happy in their own final days) but ended up throwing in as a bonus "dessert" once it was clear that Homer was *still* hungry even after the chicken, canned food, and sardines had been dispatched.

All in, five-pound Homer had put away roughly the same quantity of food over the span of ninety minutes that I (more than twenty-five times Homer's weight, it should be noted) typically consumed over the course of an entire Thanksgiving Day.

"His appetite's been pretty good," I told the vet. "If anything, he's been eating more enthusiastically than usual."

"That's great!" There was a note of surprise in her voice, but she quickly moved on to the next concern. "We should also talk about the best way to manage Homer's discomfort." By *discomfort* I knew she meant *pain.* "With his numbers, I'd expect to see him experiencing some fairly extreme discomfort. We can talk about a few medications that could make his end-of-life care less stressful for you both."

The numbers, the numbers . . . I'd managed to forget those wretched numbers for all of five minutes, but here they were again—razor-sharp in their cold, ironclad inevitability. I was living in a fool's paradise, preparing to light holiday candles and happily noting things like Homer's "swagger" and healthy appetite. As if those kinds of intangibles mattered at all in the face of the stern reality of THE NUMBERS.

"We should try to keep Homer as comfortable as possible," the vet added.

At that moment, Homer streaked past with Clayton's belled collar dangling from his mouth, filling the room with the merry jingle-jangle of sleigh bells as he triumphantly tossed his head and the collar along with it. The kittens' ringing collars had originally been intended as an early-warning system, to give Homer a heads-up when a kitten was approaching. But anything with bells attached was, as far as Homer was concerned, a fascinating cat toy and therefore his own special property. Accordingly, he'd pinned poor Clayton down in the other room and wrested the breakaway collar from around Clayton's neck. And Clayton—who hated wearing the darn thing, but was perversely outraged at having it stolen—bunny-hopped after Homer as fast as his three legs would carry him, frantically (and futilely) trying to snatch it back.

"I mean . . ." I trailed off, not wanting to sound like someone in complete denial of medical realities, but also unsure how to explain the scene in front of me, in any convincing fashion, to a doctor whose voice rang with genuine concern for a cat she clearly believed was in his final throes.

"Homer doesn't seem *un*comfortable," I finally concluded.

Having taken a few victory laps up and down the hallway, Homer bounded back into the living room and—in two swift leaps as graceful and sure-footed as a gazelle's—sprang from the floor to the dining table, and from the table to the kitchen counter next to me, before dropping the collar next to my hand. Then he jumped back down to the floor to sit in front of me, ears up at full attention. *Throw it!* his entire posture begged.

Clayton, panting slightly from his fruitless attempt at keeping up with Homer, entered a few steps behind. Indignation burned in the golden eyes he fixed on my own. *Are you just gonna* let *him rob me like that?!*

"Well, be sure to keep a close eye on him, and call if you see any changes," the vet said. "With cats, especially, the signs of discomfort can be very subtle."

I moved toward the kitchen entrance that faced the hallway and tossed the collar high in the air. It landed at the far end of the hall, and Homer was after it like a shot.

"I absolutely will," I assured her. "And thank you so much for calling. Truly."

Clayton continued to stare at me accusingly as I hung up the phone. "Let Homer have it," I bent down to tell him as I stroked his back. "He's very, *very* sick."

It didn't sound entirely persuasive to my own ears, and Clayton certainly wasn't buying it. He continued to hop after me, squeaking in protest at the injustice of it all, as I walked back into the kitchen. It was only after I'd bribed him with a small handful of Greenies that he finally relented.

Let me add here that I didn't think then—and don't think now—that the doctors were wrong in their diagnosis of Homer. I never believed that they'd overestimated the severity of Homer's condition in a fit of hubris or blind rush to judgment, that they didn't have an accurate scientific grasp of what they were looking at, or that they'd carelessly managed to mix up Homer's lab results with some other poor cat's.

I did ask to have Homer's blood retested by a different lab, only because the numbers (liver values *fifteen hundred* percent higher than normal!) seemed so outrageous that it felt irresponsible *not* to give them a second look. When I proposed the retest, my vet agreed immediately. *I'll be honest, I've never seen anything like this,* is what she said at the time. *It really shouldn't be possible.*

But even if the numbers hadn't been confirmed by the second lab (which they were), and even if this hadn't been the trusted veterinary clinic that had provided informed, compassionate care for all five of my cats over the past ten years (which it was), it still would have been clear that something wasn't entirely right with Homer. Exhibit A was his yellow—or, at least, yellow*ing*—gums and ears, irrefutable indicators of liver disease. Exhibit B was the thing that had brought us rushing pell-mell to the animal hospital in the first place: the fact that Homer had fainted. He'd actually *fainted away*, fallen down unconscious, right in front of me. There was simply no way to explain away a thing like that as "normal" or unremarkable. *Something* had caused it—and if it had brought down a cat of Homer's stamina (the magnitude of which we were coming to appreciate more each day), that *something* had to be fairly significant.

Numbers are math, and math is certainty. Homer's numbers were what they were; there was no getting around it. And yet, wasn't the world filled with examples of numbers being imprecise, when the very best minds using the most technologically advanced

32

predictive tools still hadn't managed to foresee the right outcome? How to explain those seven thousand untrained rebels defeating a battle-tested army of fifty thousand? How to explain oil that was enough to burn for only one day but nonetheless burned for eight? How to explain the very idea of Christmas miracles, which had persisted for more than a thousand years? What was a "miracle" anyway, if not an instance in which science and logic said one thing, but life ended up saying something else?

I light the Hanukkah candles every year and recite the ritual blessing over them, but I'll admit that I've never been much for genuine prayer. Nevertheless, that year I sent out a thought each night as Laurence and I lit the menorah—a silent supplication to whoever or whatever might be listening. *Let Homer be as the Hanukkah flame and burn eight times longer than he's supposed to,* I pleaded. *And if that's too much to ask, then let him still be here on Christmas. Give me one more Christmas and New Year's with Homer, and I'll be satisfied.*

We made much of Homer that holiday season. As Homer's appetite continued to go up instead of down, Laurence was tireless in his quest to find new and intriguing things to bring home for Homer's daily meals. And it seemed as if I couldn't hold or cuddle Homer enough—couldn't dig out enough toys to throw for him or find too many hours in the day to play another spirited round of Attack Mom's Fingers Under The Bedsheet.

I'd held off on stringing the holiday lights around our apartment, unable to shake the (admittedly irrational) idea that if I stopped the outward signs of the holidays' approach, I could also stop time itself and keep Homer with me longer. But when the eight nights of Hanukkah plus two additional days had come and gone—when Homer's two-week deadline and bottle of medication had both run out—with Homer showing no signs of flagging in strength or spirit, I finally decided to untangle the holiday lights from their dusty repose in the corner of a closet. This was my first, cautious step toward moving the clock forward again. With or without my superstitions, Homer didn't seem to be going anywhere.

Homer, as he did every year, engaged in his cherished ritual of snarling himself in the string of lights thoroughly, until it was impossible for me to continue hanging them up without first dislodging him. But instead of my usual impatient cry of, *Homer, enough already!* I told him, "Just be careful, Homer-Bear. You're a good boy."

I couldn't keep the crack out of my voice. The unmistakable sorrow in my tone—which was most decidedly *not* a regular part of our holiday tradition—couldn't have stopped Homer more abruptly in his tracks than if I'd yelled at him harshly and chased him from the room. He'd been rolling around on the floor but swiftly sat upright, ears at attention as his head moved in the sweeping, sonar-dish motion that meant he was trying to understand something he couldn't see yet still knew was happening around him.

Wait a second, he seemed to be saying. *What's going on? Why aren't you getting mad at me like you normally do?*

It wasn't as if Homer could look at the calendar and note that the lights were going up later than usual, or overhear conversations I had with his doctor and understand what we were talking about. But, still . . . he knew that something was different this year.

We spent a quiet Christmas Eve at home with Chinese takeout from the place across the street. Little more than glorified fast food, this particular restaurant was never my own first choice. But Homer—always an eager eater, if not a discerning one—practically did backflips for their five-dollar chicken breast.

(I mean that literally, by the way. Smelling the chicken, sealed in its container, the moment Laurence stepped off the elevator—through our closed apartment door and all the way down the hall—Homer was leaping so ecstatically by the time Laurence finally walked in that he knocked askew two paintings hanging a full five feet off the ground. Our downstairs neighbor called to complain about the noise.)

Scrapping among the discarded wrappings from the after-dinner gifts Laurence and I exchanged, Clayton and Homer engaged in a fast and furious round of tug-of-war over a snippet of ribbon, while Fanny—who, as the only cat in the house with four legs and two eyes, might actually have won if she'd decided to play—opted instead to throttle one of her new toy mice into submission.

I knew it was absurd—that I was descending into full-on "helicopter parent" obsessiveness—but I started to go over to Homer and Clayton, to interfere in their game on Homer's behalf. With time running so short for him, I wanted Homer to have whatever he wanted, even if all he wanted was a lousy piece of used holiday ribbon.

"Don't." Laurence put a hand on my arm to hold me back. "After fifteen years, don't start treating him like he's 'special' now."

Homer had sensed that I was standing up and turned his head in my direction. He'd been especially attuned to my every movement these past few weeks, which I knew was because I'd been so hypervigilant of him that I'd made him self-conscious. Now, as I distracted Homer just long enough for Clayton to successfully pry the scrap of ribbon away from him, I realized that Laurence was right. I had no idea what, against all the odds, had been keeping Homer so buoyant for so long. But I did know that—as with any legendary fighter or athlete—self-doubt was the one thing that would bring him crashing down.

Christmas morning was hard for me. Logically, it shouldn't have been. I'd made a wish over the candles at Hanukkah, and I'd gotten exactly what I'd wished for: Homer was still with me. Better yet, there was nothing (aside from a few conclusive medical tests and the consensus of his doctors) to indicate that he was going anywhere anytime soon.

Nevertheless, it was hardly an exaggeration to say that I'd barely left the house for more than half an hour at a time since Homer's fateful hospital visit three weeks earlier. A dinner with out-of-town friends was all I'd managed, and those two hours away from my home and my Homer-Bear had been agonizing.

Laurence and I had planned to spend Christmas Day with family and friends in New Jersey—an annual tradition that I always looked forward to. But we'd be away for eight or nine hours, at least. Maybe even longer. And suddenly, standing in front of the closet with my head tangled in a sweater as I got dressed that morning, I didn't think I could go through with it. What if something happened while I was gone? What if there was another fainting episode, or some equally dire emergency?

What if Homer left me for good, and I wasn't even there to say goodbye?

Tears had risen many times since I'd first spoken with Homer's doctor three weeks back; a few had even fallen. Still, I hadn't actually cried. I didn't cry very often, and I didn't intend to start now—not when I was supposed to be out the door and on my way to a festive holiday gathering that I was already running late for.

For once, however, I was unable to keep my tears at bay. Collapsing onto the bed, I curled up on my side, buried my face in a pillow, and sobbed.

Homer was on the bed, too—keeping me company while I got dressed, as he always did. You could probably count on one hand the number of times Homer had heard me cry over the course of our years together. But when it did happen, it was something that always bothered him. Tentatively, as if he feared that a faster approach might cause alarm, he crept across the bed toward me.

The first time I'd met Homer, fifteen years earlier—in the office of the idealistic young vet who'd saved his life, on a sunny Miami afternoon when Homer was only a two-week-old kitten passed over time and again by potential adopters—the very first thing he'd done was to climb up the front of my sweater until he'd reached the crook of my neck. Once there, he'd nestled himself in and proceeded to purr his little heart out against my ear.

It was a gesture he'd go on to repeat many times in the months that followed, but hadn't done in the fourteen-plus years since he'd reached his adult size. Small as Homer was when he was fully grown, he was still too big to fit comfortably in the gap between my shoulder and my jaw.

Now, however, climbing carefully across my curled-up form, that was exactly what he did. It was an awkward fit, and I raised one hand to help steady him. The warmth of Homer's body in the space just above my heart felt every bit as good as it had back then. The thrum of his purr against my ear was as strong and joyful as it had ever been in all the years since.

"I love you, Homer-Bear," I murmured into the black softness of his fur.

We'd made promises to each other, Homer and I, back on that first day, in that very first moment, when we'd decided without words that we would belong to each other from then on. And I knew—now, here, in this moment—that he was making a promise to me again.

With infinite gentleness, Homer brought his face to mine and began licking the tears, one by one, from my cheeks.

Believe, I imagined him saying.

The doctors had told us that Homer had two weeks left, at most. But the flame that supposedly had only enough oil to last for fourteen days would go on to burn—bright and true—for another nine months.

And Homer and I were together for all of it, right up until the very last moment. But, long before that moment came, I learned again what I'd always known: that nobody could tell Homer what his potential was. That nobody—not all the doctors in the world, and certainly not me—had any business telling Homer what he could or couldn't do, or trying to prevent him from living every day of his life to the absolute fullest, in his own way, on his own terms.

That Homer lived as long as he did—when nothing in the lab results or medical textbooks could account for such a thing—was a miracle. Life in the face of hopelessness is always a miracle. Every day you get to spend with someone you love is a miracle in its own right.

And then there are the extra days—the ones you never thought you'd get but are somehow lucky enough to have anyway with your very best friend by your side. Those are the greatest miracles of all.

ABOUT THE AUTHOR

Gwen Cooper is the *New York Times* bestselling author of the memoirs *Homer's Odyssey: A Fearless Feline Tale, or How I Learned About Love and Life with a Blind Wonder Cat; Homer: The Ninth Life of a Blind Wonder Cat;* and *My*  *Life in a Cat House: True Tales of Love, Laughter, and Living with Five Felines;* as well as the novel *Love Saves the Day*, narrated from a cat's point of view. She also writes the Curl Up with a Cat Tale monthly short-story series about the ongoing adventures of her "fur kids." Her work has been published in nearly two dozen languages. She's a frequent speaker at shelter fundraisers and donates 10 percent of her royalties from *Homer's Odyssey* to organizations that serve abused, abandoned, and disabled pets. Gwen lives in New Jersey with her husband, Laurence. She also lives with her two perfect cats—Clayton "the Tripod" and his littermate, Fanny—who aren't impressed with any of it.

Want more Cat Tales?

Don't miss Gwen Cooper's Curl Up with a Cat Tale series!

I Choo-Choo-Choose You!

Stop Trying to Make Fetch Happen

The Picasso of Pee

Cat Carrier Tango

THEM!

Fanny Trouble

Check out the "Curl Up with a Cat Tale" short story subscription series at gwencooper.com/cattales.

Want more Cat Tales?

Don't miss Gwen Cooper's *My Life in a Cat House*!

Collected from the *Curl Up with a Cat Tale* series

My Life *in* a Cat House

True Tales of Love, Laughter, and Living with Five Felines

GWEN COOPER

New York Times bestselling author of *Homer's Odyssey*

Celebrate the human-feline bond with all its joys, mysteries, and life-changing moments.

Gwen Cooper returns with the ongoing adventures of her much-beloved, world-famous fur family. Ideal for new readers and longtime fans alike, this collection of eight *purr*-fect cat stories is filled with all the humor and heart Gwen's devoted readership has come to know and love.

Read all eight stories in one sitting, or savor each gem of a "tail" on its own. *My Life in a Cat House* will leave you laughing out loud, shedding an occasional tear, and hugging your own cat a little bit closer.

Check out the "Curl Up with a Cat Tale" short story subscription series at gwencooper.com/cattales.